MAGMA

POEMS

LUCÍA ARROCHA

Copyright © 2025 by Lucía Arrocha.

All rights reserved.

First paperback edition September 2025

Photography by Ioannis Charalambidis
Cover design by Lucía Arrocha
Cover photography by Ioannis Charalambidis
Author portrait by Quinn Miller-Bedell

ISBN 979-8-218-74416-8 (paperback)
Library of Congress Control Number: 2025915759
LC record available at https://lccn.loc.gov/2025915759

Published by Umbra Press in San Francisco, CA.

For every part of you that is destined for the surface.

Thank you Celina, Toya and Zehara for generously reading every poem I've written from 2020-2024 and helping me with this selection.

CONTENTS

Vantage 9

Las almas juegan de noche 11

Light 12

Hands 13

Projections 14

Predicciones 15

I speak to you 17

I look forward to the silence 18

Verano 21

Offer 22

Nascent 23

Multiplicity 25

Omen 27

Broken mirror 29

Noise 31

Fidelidad 32

Brimming soon 33

Invisible hands 34

Franqueza 35

Receta para el insomnio 37

Pavement 39

Axis 40

Muscle memory 41

Lmk 42

Onus	43
Crumbs	45
Phantasmagoria	47
Folds	48
Quicksand	49
Stuck	51
Merit	52
On life and strategy	53
Mining	54
To watch it break	55
Sandía	57
Knives of a generation	58
Bird out of context	60
False bottom	61
Cartesian plane	62
Come visit	63
Trece	65
Go to the sage	66
Sunshine	67
Hélice	69
Ciao	71
A clearing	73
Eight of swords	75
I will bury you slowly	77
Homeostasis	79
There she is!	81
About the Author	83

MAGMA

Vantage

The melodies the wind

Will sing

In the walk between

Two blades of grass,

A lifetime couldn't read

The full story

Of a teardrop;

A story that reaches the ocean

And becomes everyone's,

Rolling indelible.

Las almas juegan de noche

Bienvenida la noche,
La calle de luz teñida,
El alma despierta
Al hallarme dormida

Y cobra anclaje en lo hondo,
Mientras el cuerpo entumece,
Se aventura a respirar
Entre los peces.

Fuera ya la noción de tiempo,
Cuenta sólo el placer
De irse en lo alto,
Junto al viento, a correr.

Bienvenida el alba,
Las almas, del cielo tendidas,
Inician su febril retorno
Y amanecen perdidas.

Light

Wanderer,

How many worlds do you know?

What a collection

You've carried through,

Enabled

Destroyed

Suffered

Enjoyed,

Your tendrils

Touch

That which cannot meet

Itself,

Even beyond

The confines

Of its deepest imagination,

Yet the affect sustains

And you pour yourself

Over everything

That's worth seeing

And otherwise too;

All of life

Starts with you.

Hands

My hands don't seem to be
Feeling out for contours,
You don't seem to have
Anything in mind,
What a lovely coincidence
We find ourselves
Intertwined.

Projections

Sometimes I'll get tempted
To reach out
And pull at your skin
To unravel the places
And people you've been,
Build an archive of your thoughts,
Sit in patches of sun
And read your story for hours,
Seeking out your building blocks,
The deepest secrets I'd unlock,
I'd show my allegiance
By not saying a word
And helping you carry
The weight of your world.

Predicciones

Sería poco razonable,

Ahora,

Presumir

Que nos conocemos,

Mas aún los sedimentos

Que establecen

Mis recuerdos

Te conciernen,

Te considero,

Y vernos

No nos parecerá

Nada nuevo.

I speak to you,

In a forgotten language
That voyages the air,
Traverses the water
In the form of a small pulse,

When it reaches you
Can you feel it?

We correspond
Through thoughts,
In private delights,
Memories that spark,
That we hold,
That we share,
As we send out warmth
And shapes of hope
For one another,
In an old language,
Out of earshot,
Subdermal.

I look forward to the silence,

In walking down the street
Stopping in front of a flower shop
To check out the shapes
That gestures and promises take;
Efforts that speak in color,

In sitting at a table,
Maybe we're holding hands,
Maybe we're just sharing space,
Your back leaning low against this chair
As I think you'd do
When you have no demands to tend to,
Real or imagined,

And I'm immersed
In my cup of tea,
Or looking out,
Maybe my hand is on your knee,
Settling in from the long walk,
The hills climbed,
The thresholds crossed
Of our intimacies,
Into the first rest,
In quiet confidence,
Blueprint in place

For the sediments of presence
To take it from here,
Now that our choice is made,
Now that some heavy lifting is done
And we remain.

Verano

Cuando las tardes se vuelven largas
Y la brisa suspira entre tus dedos,
Carantoñas de mediados de febrero

La luz naranja
Colada por el mosquitero
Se vuelca sobre el pasto,
Y el bullicio oscuro
De las cigarras
Entre los jazmines

Cuando te mordés el labio,
Pensante,
Todo tu foco
Intentando
Ver el otro lado.

Offer

What have you
Kind one
To offer?

What say you
My dear
You'd give?

Where exactly
Is it
Within me
You'd like
To live?

Is it even
Possible
To discern
Between any sort of love
And any form
Of its return?

Nascent

One day,

I hope to put my hand on your shoulder

With the authority to do so

Today I notice how shyly

My fingers inquire

Along your neck,

How I wish I knew it better

As the noise from the window

Hollows you out

And I have nothing in my pocket

To say,

But how I wish—

How I wish I did.

Multiplicity

Can't really

Put my finger on it,

Is it the many?

Is it which many?

What makes it,

More or less,

The very nature

Of you?

Where is

The common thread

That outlines

Every facet

It combines,

Allotting the space

Within the confines

It permits

To be true;

What does it take,

How much is allowed

To be you?

Omen

I had a dream of air,
Walking down the corridor
To find you standing there
As I knew you would,

Embers of despair
As we suspected we shouldn't
Yet wondered if we could,
Then flooded in the water,
Crept up to our knees,
We never discussed the matter;
One thinks not of what one sees,

So the ground begins to shatter
Draining our sullen minds,
Leaving nothing but the earth
And our fantasies behind,

Not the prudent nor the wise
Can gracefully unwind
The ever-knotted surprise
Of your shadow passing by.

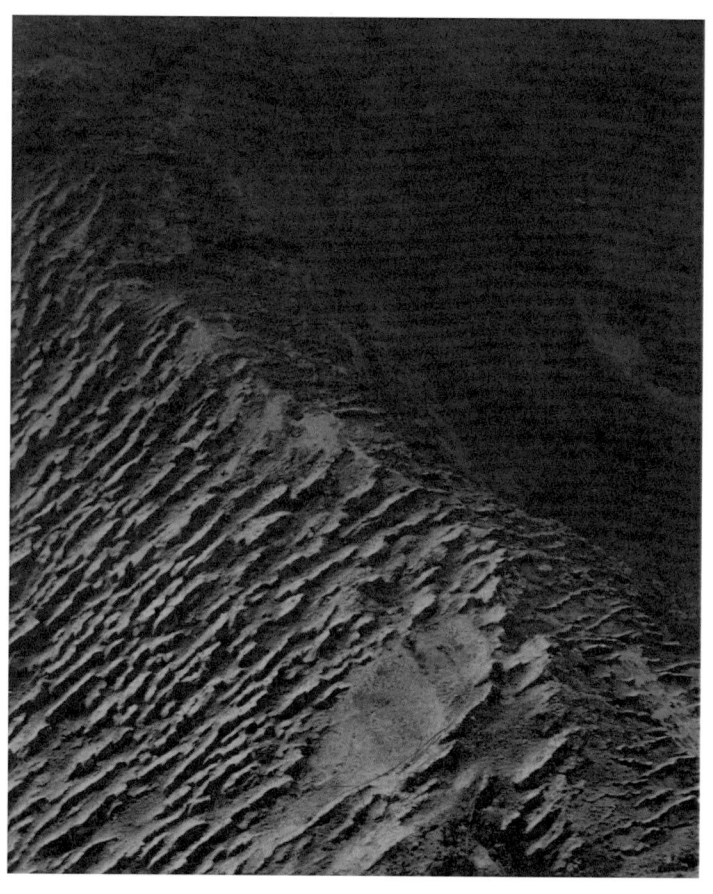

Broken mirror

How does one move forward
Without kicking back,
How can one sleep after
Exposing what they lack?

Crack that chest wide open,
Tricks of the trade,
But, truthfully, I'm afraid
Of myself.

How many steps onward
Can leave one satisfied,
To rest their tired legs
And not be mauled by dread,
But feel their leisure justified?

Spill the thought that's aching,
For it is not engraved,
But, truthfully, I'm just afraid.

Noise

Trying to separate

The signal from the noise

Pulling at

The weeds in your voice,

Receptors optimize

For high fidelity

Meanwhile my faith

Is weary,

I wonder if I can

Open this door

And receive the question

As it's meant to be heard,

Playing with the template,

The thought projecting

Into my sense of self understanding,

In the hope to rework structures

Without obliterating foundations,

Without tunneling through introspection,

Am I in the way of seeing?

Are you in the way of showing?

Receptors optimize for high fidelity

My inner voice decanting…

Fidelidad

Equivocarse
Es natural.
Serán las herramientas;
A saber.

El errar
Que no alerta dormidos,
Sesgados, por
La proximidad
Representando lo veraz
En esta narrativa

Si te hago caso
Y apago ese filtro
Me quedo
Mas quemo, dormida.

Brimming soon

There is no unequivocal good,
Only measures of it,
Consider the trees
The air
And seas,
All of it,
Their measures of good
Striving not to starve
Nor to overwhelm
And banish everything else
To the underside,

When do you think,
If not already,
Our measure will be up?
Are we still moving,
Are we still learning,
Where does the water
Outline our cup?

Invisible hands,

Sight unseen
Pulling at us
Claiming ignorance
Comfortably
Resting on the imperial laurels
Of empirical evidence

What a spectacle;
Trees unheard,
How dare you say
They are not fallen?
Hearts unfelt,
Nonetheless left bleeding
Forgotten
Crying
Calling.

Franqueza

De franqueza temeraria
Y demás cuestiones,
Los pies echando raíces,
La boca floreciendo en palabras
Picantes como abejas,
Crepitando en oídos fugaces

Tan dóciles nos movemos
Al inhalar, ofrecer el pecho,
Dejar al veneno atravesar,
Qué curioso ejercicio complejo
Que a diario damos por hecho,
Un acto de amor
Es ver al daño
Mirarlo a los ojos
Y dejarlo pasar.

Receta para el insomnio

Perfume de cortisol
I woke up in a sweat
Circunloquio around my rib cage
Tirante tirante
Makes it hard to breathe
Pensante pensante
Quedarse o tachar
Cuestiones pendientes

Bocanadas
Entre sumergidas
Parecerían ser
Increasingly menos
Frecuentes
Menos
Hondas
El mareo
Takes over
Y otorga a la marea
The upper hand.

Quisiera soltarle el bozal
Ultimately aprender
A reparar
Sin ser indistinto
Abandonar al instinto
De reprender.

Pavement

As the pavement unfolds

Beneath my feet

And I lean

Against the light post,

It flickers,

My skin, textured

by the rain,

I remember

I had promised to quit

But the smoke

Prevails,

Distant melodies

Of yours,

Of them,

And I recall

Thinking,

Wishing,

Wrongly,

Thinking it'd be different,

That I'd be safer,

If you never

Wrote about me.

Axis

Considering love as a word,
It is not just a noun,

Now far beyond
What could withstand,
Left to no devices
But to lower
One's arms,
Beyond the extent
Of how I could
Romance you,
I denounce you
On the axis of the verb.

Muscle memory

This body does not forget
This body does not forgive
And it demands
That which it's learned to get

My arms remember
The angles of your hold,
My chest will curve
To the shape of your spine,
My lips, unprompted,
Kick off the dance
Of calling you mine.

Lmk

I don't want to assume
That there's enough of you
For me
To consume.

Onus

In the grip

Of the body inconsolable

I remember

There are forces that fight for me

There are forces that fight against me

My only power

Is to show my favor.

Crumbs

El andar
Se complicaría
Al parecer
Cada queja
Una bala
Al pie
Y no quiero quedarme
Con las migas

Es la distancia
Kilométrica
En mis pupilas
Lamentable forma
De realizar
Aquel fin fatal

Me cuesta
Desarmar
Me cuesta
Conectar
No quiero ser las migas
Entre todas
Tus amigas.

Phantasmagoria

How easy it is,

Hidden immobility,

The stare

Unraveled,

Unfocused,

Empty,

Still,

How still,

So still,

Toward nothing,

Maybe a flicker,

But quickly stifled,

Heaven forbid

Any sort,

Any semblance

Of an awakening,

Maybe perhaps

In humor,

But only

Of the utmost

Levity.

Folds,

Come undone,
Currents,
Like threads,
Weaving motions,
Unraveling trails,
Floating sensations,
Finding impact still,

To hover
And, in a moment,
Look up
At the distance
From where we started;
One-way threads,
Paths departed.

Quicksand

I,
The mark you left
Is fading

I,
The cup of coffee you made
grows colder

I,
Your scent on my sweater
Is dissolving

I,
Your laughter pours
Into silence

I,
I'm not going to sleep
I'm just
I'm just resting my eyes
For a bit.

Stuck

Doesn't quite feel like stuck
Or, rather, it's harder to notice
When, to begin with, you're rigid,
Lungs frozen, mid exhale,
In their bodice

What choices await,
What can movement budge?
The loss,
The sludge;
Consequences today,
An avalanche too many,
Does the forest fire
Still require
This bucket, at best,
Half empty?

In the mechanics of resilience
Would it heal or hinder
To find depth or reason
In carrying on?
What gains stem from belief
As one proceeds,
If any?
Should I've had that
In me
Already?

Merit

To some, what matters most
Is the simplest term
But in our hearts we host
Trust only in complexity.

How can substance
And ease coexist?
The flesh is weak
And merit blossoms
From what is difficult to speak.

On life and strategy

It still remains unclear

Whether it matters at this juncture

To traverse the fear

Whether there is value at all

In deciding to have hope

In the midst of all this grief

To search for the light

Through the smoke

To rebel in disbelief

Refuse what is

And charge towards what could be

Whilst dragging deep uncertainty

The perpetual dread all too near;

It still remains unclear.

Mining

Seems like you're doing a lot,
Don't get me wrong,
But it's a lot
Of the wrong thing?

Now the rocks pile up everywhere
And your arms are tired
From all the sweeping,
Your rug is big,
But not that big,
And mining hurts
But lasts.

To watch it break,

It's too easy,
The energy is minor,
Fingers spread
And gravity
Drives the course,
Hands falsely tied therefore

I fear I'd be a coward
To let it swallow
And holding
Could, someday,
Not poison
Not burn,
Yet those claws
Are uncertain,
It's a bargain
But how easy
What a bore
To release
And behold
What's been done before.

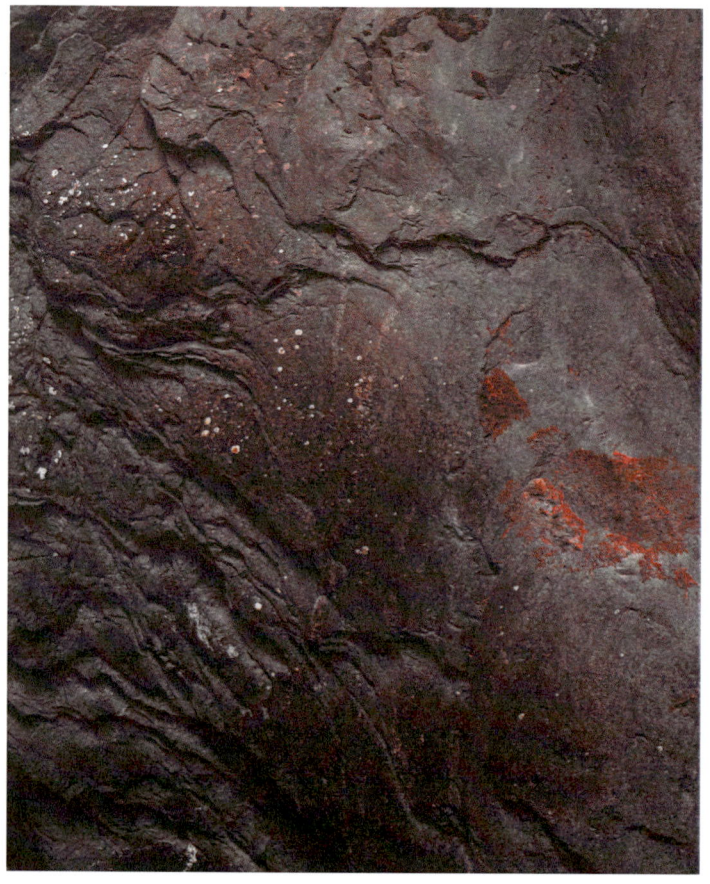

Sandía

Todos los nudos
En la garganta
En la boca del estómago
Se juntan a bailar
A la luz de la luna,
Los dedos
Sobre un cráneo
Que apenas reconozco

La migraña
De rogar identidad,
Las úlceras
De la hambruna,
El cráneo
Expuesto
No es mío,
El descanso
Tampoco.

Knives of a generation

I suspect we value
Our past more than our future,
For the past is the only thing
That's guaranteed to us;
A false ground,
Just as fictitious,
But ground nonetheless.

Why else would we compete
With our present,
Claiming it all the more terrible,
And the generations that were youth before us,
Pull out their knives in defense
Of a fear that, at the time,
Was just as visceral to them,
That has long since left scars
Like cage bars,
Now blindfolds
Invisible to them,
But we weren't there
So we "wouldn't understand",

And, in their years of armor,
Condescend
Upon us now,
Shell-less

And afraid,

Of the horrors that are,

And the worse peeking its head

Around the corner

With a triumphant grin,

As we prioritize

Pitting the horses of the past

And present against one another,

In a race, immaterial,

Like the future we so avoid

To work towards.

Bird out of context

Thought I knew who I was,
But this bird revealed itself,
Out of context,
And then so was I.
In that scream I found myself
Unidentified.

The mirror has ripples in it
From the question I threw at it,
Now it's just pouring over
Pieces I don't need.

The walls seem closer,
The bird's eyes grow wider,
It's losing all its feathers,
And it blankly stares at me.

One arm arrows through its pupil,
Something pulls me from within,
I allow without resistance:
Shedding gladly this old skin.

False bottom

To step into
A puddle, head on,
And feel the blood rush up
As a black hole swallows,
Revealing the ocean
Concealed in the shadows.

Cartesian plane

In shock
And in youth
Was how it was for me,
Not so for the rest
Of my friends' families,
Where Chance
Took a promenade
Across the cartesian plane
Of age and health,

And now we are four,
Our fathers out the door,
The committee which I preside
Is a source of pain as it is of pride,
These winding archives
For our survival
I derive.

Come visit

To the love
That lingers:
I sleep often,
Come visit
Sometime.

Trece

Como una gran novela

Te recuerdo con el tiempo

En sentimientos

Por sobre hechos

Tu impacto más que tu historia

Tu risa,

Lamento,

Se amarillenta con los años

Y mis manotazos de ahogado

A memorias de memorias

A fotos incrementalmente crípticas

Y querer resistir, inútil,

A mis pasos tomados

Que sin duda te alejan

De mi presente,

Afecto indeleble

Memoria decreciente.

Go to the sage,

With feline precision
They will offer a vision
To relinquish the strain
Of someone beloved
Dissolved now his name
In the depths of what was
But holy still today
In the eye of the heart
And the heart of the mind
Your presence persists
I'm as yours
As you are mine
And in your memory
I vow to stay kind.

Sunshine

Hello, sunshine,
What say you
About the day that's warming?

Peeling back the layers
Of your sister's warning;
The glowing speckles
Dissolve with you.

I remember someone said
You are ever-glowing
With such effervescent faith,
I wonder if they knew
Even you shall be replaced?

Hélice

Alguna vez me dijeron
Que el paso del tiempo
Es helicoidal:
Dependiendo del ángulo
Por el cual mires
Avanzamos mas volvemos
Al mismo lugar

Fijate qué curiosidad
Una década mirando hacia delante
Asumiendo una línea recta
Me toma desapercibidamente
Reiterarnos de manera tal
Qué regalo y qué belleza
Después de tanta vida
Después de tanto mar
Querernos, aún,
En circunferencia
Y poco azar.

Ciao

I ran into you last night
In a dream
I was surprised,
Delighted
And saddened
To see you.
Like a good girl,
I kept it to myself
Because I heard you
When you spoke your terms;
It would be awful
To pretend I hadn't,

To miss you, unfortunately,
Allows me not the ability
To say "this is news to me"
In earnest and without consequence

But I can mope about it here,
In the privacy of my thoughts;
That, when I see you,
I wish I could share with you
My defeats and triumphs,
Rekindle reality
Rather than
This expanding memory
Between us.

A clearing

The skin alerts
A clearing,
The temperature drops
A few degrees;
Briskness,
Counterintuitively,
Frees.

One mustn't indulge,
The möbius depleted;
To forget
This beautiful nightmare
Is to repeat it.

Eight of swords

It takes so much
And, sometimes,
Fortunately, nothing at all

To shrink your
Weight
To the proportions
Of this earth

The world is so big

It is so, that
The sword pointed
At my chest
Is foley

It is so, that
The wind
That rattles my hinges
Hangs from strings

The world is so big

It is so that,
In all its vastness,
You don't touch me.

I will bury you slowly,

Feel every inch of clay
Tint my hands,
Adhere to what wasn't,
Cover that which couldn't;
I will not hide away

You carry so much sadness
in your fugitive body,
Latent, it accumulates
Until the weight stuns

Where will you turn to
then, immobilized,
Blinders still in frame?
I am just one
Of the links you add
To elongate your chains.

Homeostasis

All my neuroses are coming out,
I think it's the proximity,
So thanks for bearing with me
As I sort them out

Is this a corner that I'm turning
Or the crest of a sine wave?
I'm not sure but, just in case,
I'm recording every milestone, babe.

There she is!

It's good to see you happy,
Clock that grin from across the room
As you tie up your hair,

I know it's been a while,
The creases around your mouth
Recall the position,
How they missed it,

How they missed you so,
Funny and playing,
Shoulders had forgotten
They could rest so low
As if oblivious to the fact
That they weren't before,

Darling grin, reach out;
Show me those teeth
That delight
In whatever today
Is on about.

About the Author

Lucía Arrocha is Chilean born, Argentine raised and San Francisco based. She has been writing poetry for over two decades.

Her multicultural background has fostered in her a proclivity for language, as well as a profound fascination with different ways of living and emoting.

When she is not writing she can be found tending to her friendships, fawning over her cats, Jasper and Oliver, or selecting tracks on the dance floor.

www.ingramcontent.com/pod-product-compliance
Lightning Source LLC
Chambersburg PA
CBRC101143030426
42337CB00007B/60